Twisters
A Book About Tornadoes

by Rick Thomas   illustrated by Denise Shea

Content Adviser: Daniel Dix, Senior Meteorologist,
The Weather Channel

Reading Adviser: Susan Kesselring, M.A., Literacy Educator,
Rosemount-Apple Valley-Eagan (Minnesota) School District

PICTURE WINDOW BOOKS
Minneapolis, Minnesota

Managing Editor: Catherine Neitge
Creative Director: Terri Foley
Art Director: Keith Griffin
Editor: Patricia Stockland
Designer: Nathan Gassman
Page production: Picture Window Books
The illustrations in this book were prepared digitally.

Picture Window Books
5115 Excelsior Boulevard
Suite 232
Minneapolis, MN 55416
877-845-8392
www.picturewindowbooks.com

Copyright © 2005 by Picture Window Books
All rights reserved. No part of this book may be reproduced without
written permission from the publisher. The publisher takes no
responsibility for the use of any of the materials or methods
described in this book, nor for the products thereof.

Printed in the United States of America.

Library of Congress Cataloging-in-Publication Data

Thomas, Rick, 1954-
Twisters : a book about tornadoes / by Rick Thomas ;
illustrated by Denise Shea.
p. cm. — (Amazing science)
Includes bibliographical references and index.
ISBN 1-4048-0930-9 (hardcover)
1. Tornadoes—Juvenile literature. I. Shea, Denise,
ill. II. Title. III. Series.

QC955.2.T45 2004
551.55'3—dc22   2004019739

Table of Contents

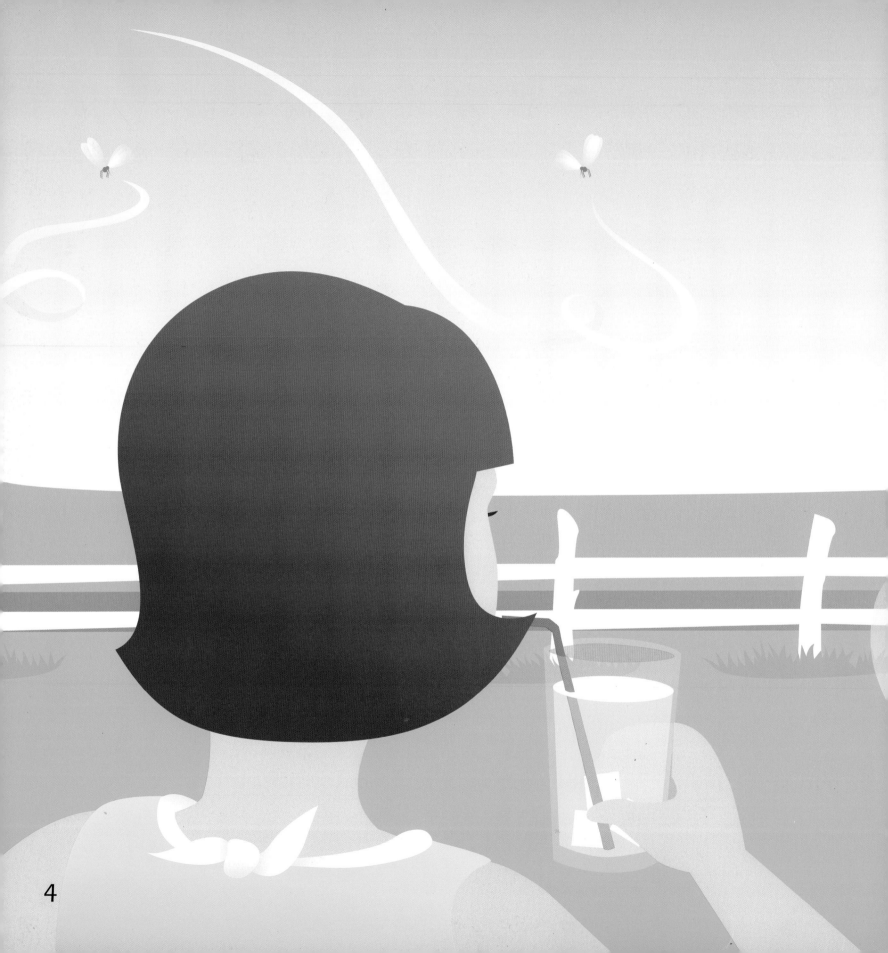

Mosquitoes buzz in the hot, sticky air. Beads of sweat roll down your back. Drops of water roll down your glass of lemonade.

Not a single cloud floats overhead. The sky is pale blue. But off to the west hangs a darker shape.

The hot, hazy, humid day is what your grandmother calls tornado weather.

Updrafts

Air is full of water vapor. Humid air feels damp and sticky. The sun heats up the humid air. The air grows warmer and warmer. The hot, moist air rises high into the sky. Huge sections of warm air that travel upward are updrafts.

Downdrafts and Thunderstorms

As water vapor rises, it mixes with higher, cooler air and expands. The vapor cools and forms tiny water droplets. Clouds form, and the droplets fall down to the ground. Rain and cool air rush downward in a large, wide mass of air called a downdraft.

Downdrafts and updrafts
rush past each other, side by side.
The busy, bustling air fills the sky with
more clouds and more rain. Soon, a
thunderstorm booms.

9

Rotation

Winds and breezes blow above Earth every day. They swirl and flow through the sky on different levels and in different directions.

In a thunderstorm, winds collide against warm updrafts. Breezes brush against cool downdrafts. The downdrafts begin to speed up as they head toward the ground. Updrafts then move faster as they rise up into the storm. These winds work together to form a rotating column of wind.

Funnel Cloud

The air cools down quickly. The sky turns green and fills with quick-moving clouds. Breezes blow the leaves. Hail falls from the clouds and bounces onto the grass.

Off to the west, a strange shape squirms out of the clouds. A dark mass that looks like a giant, spinning ice-cream cone pushes toward the ground. Below the cone is a dust cloud stirred by the rushing air.

Tornado!

When the funnel touches the ground, it connects with the dust cloud below. The funnel turns into a full-blown tornado. It grows wider and thicker. The winds spin faster and faster. Tornado winds can reach 300 miles per hour.

Behind the first tornado, another funnel reaches out of the clouds. The funnel stretches down like a long, skinny rope. Then it fades in the air. Not all funnel clouds turn into tornadoes.

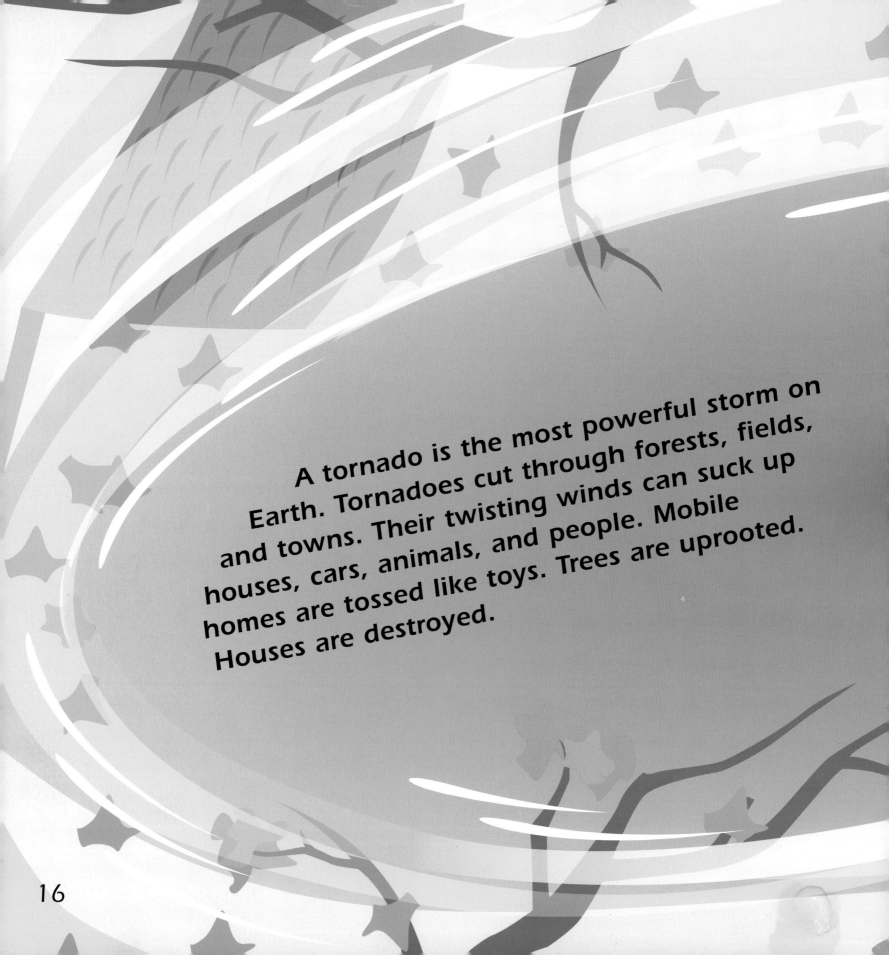

A tornado is the most powerful storm on Earth. Tornadoes cut through forests, fields, and towns. Their twisting winds can suck up houses, cars, animals, and people. Mobile homes are tossed like toys. Trees are uprooted. Houses are destroyed.

16

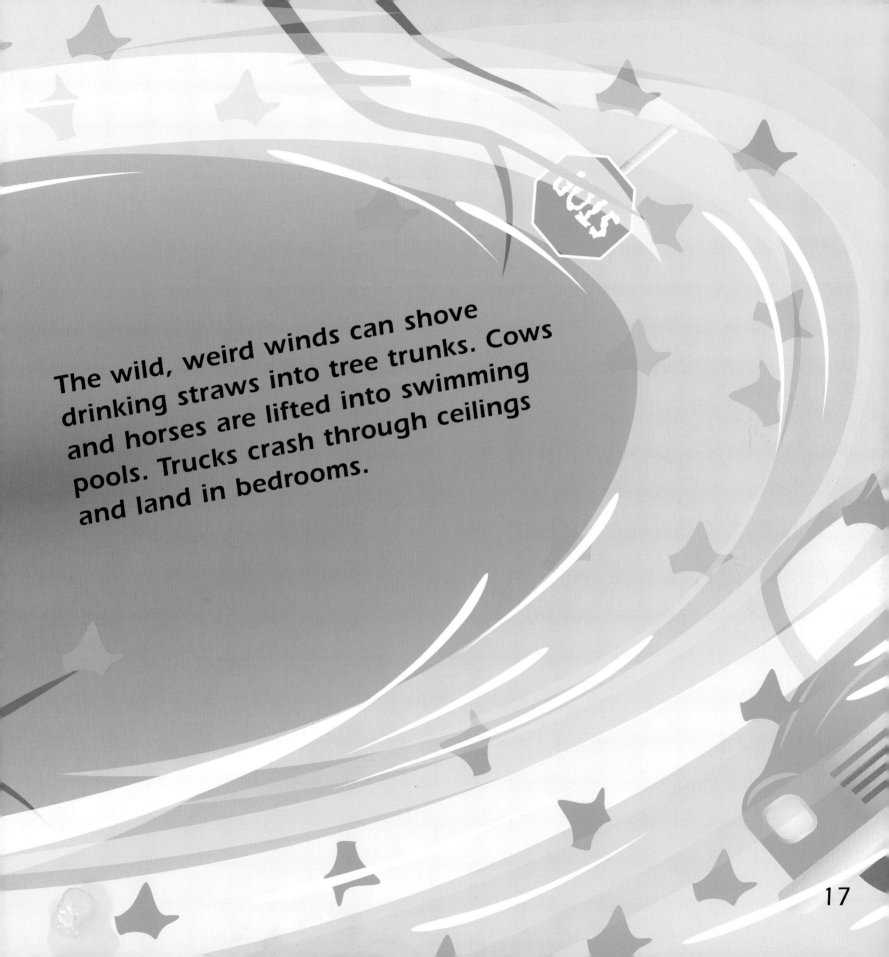

The wild, weird winds can shove drinking straws into tree trunks. Cows and horses are lifted into swimming pools. Trucks crash through ceilings and land in bedrooms.

Fast and Furious

Tornado winds sound like an invisible train roaring across the land. The howls of the storm mix with the snapping of tree branches and the groans of houses collapsing.

But the sounds fade quickly.
More than half of all tornadoes
last only 15 minutes. They
travel a mile on the ground
and then weaken. The
funnel cloud grows skinny.
It dissolves in a cloud of
dust and rain.

19

After the Tornado

Rain falls from a dark sky. The air no longer feels sticky. It's fresh and cold. Thunder rumbles as the storm moves away.

Outside are signs of damage. Roof shingles litter the grass. The porch swing is missing. But on the ground sits your undisturbed glass of lemonade. Next to it, part of the oak tree lies twisted on the lawn. A tornado can destroy everything in its path or nothing at all.

Surviving a Tornado

Don't get caught in this extreme storm. Listen to local weather stations during tornado season. Most tornadoes occur in May and June, but they can happen any time. Watch for these signs during tornado season:

- Green skies
- Quickly-moving clouds
- Hail
- A sudden calm in the middle of a noisy thunderstorm
- Funnel-shaped clouds
- An unexplainable roaring sound like a train

Stay indoors away from windows. Basements are great shelters. If an underground shelter is not available, hide under heavy furniture, such as a dining table or workbench.

Cover yourself with blankets, sleeping bags, or mattresses. These coverings will help to protect you from broken glass or other flying objects.

If you're traveling by car and a tornado is nearby, stop the car, and go lie down in a ditch. Do NOT take shelter in a highway underpass. People have been blown out of them.

Extreme Storm Extras

- Tornadoes usually form in an area that stretches from southern Minnesota and Iowa through Nebraska to Texas. This area is called "Tornado Alley."

- About 800 tornadoes are reported each year in the United States. Some weather scientists think that an extra 1,000 "weak" tornadoes develop each year but are never seen or reported.

- More tornadoes occur in the United States than in any other country.

- An outbreak is a group of six or more tornadoes that form at the same time.

- Weather forecasters help save lives by predicting bad weather and warning people before storms occur. Since 1971, no more than 50 people have been killed by a single tornado.

Glossary

dissolve—to mix with a liquid

droplets—tiny drops of water or liquid

funnel—a cone shape with an open top and bottom

hail—small, round pieces of ice that fall like rain

humid—damp or moist

rotate—rotating or spinning in a circle

sections—pieces; smaller parts of a whole

vapor—steam or mist

23

To Learn More

At the Library

Chambers, Catherine. *Tornadoes*. Chicago: Heinemann Library, 2002.

Osborne, Mary Pope. *Twister on Tuesday*. New York: Random House, 2001.

Simon, Seymour. *Tornadoes*. New York: Morrow Junior Books, 1999.

On the Web

FactHound offers a safe, fun way to find Web sites related to this book. All of the sites on FactHound have been researched by our staff. *www.facthound.com*

1. Visit the FactHound home page.
2. Enter a search word related to this book, or type in this special code: 1404809309
3. Click on the FETCH IT button.

Your trusty FactHound will fetch the best sites for you!

Index

Look for all of the books in this series:

Eye of the Storm: A Book About Hurricanes

Flakes and Flurries: A Book About Snow

Gusts and Gales: A Book About Wind

Nature's Fireworks: A Book About Lightning

Rising Waters: A Book About Floods

Rumble, Boom! A Book About Thunderstorms

Shapes in the Sky: A Book About Clouds

Sizzle! A Book About Heat Waves

Splish! Splash! A Book About Rain

Sunshine: A Book About Sunlight

Twisters: A Book About Tornadoes

Whiteout! A Book About Blizzards